Opening the Divine Treasure Chest

Opening the Divine Treasure Chest

Your Pathway into God's Presence

Eric Gilmour

DESTINY IMAGE® PUBLISHERS, INC.
P.O. Box 310, Shippensburg, PA 17257-0310
"Publishing cutting-edge prophetic resources to supernaturally empower the body of Christ"

This book and all other Destiny Image and Destiny Image Fiction books are available at Christian bookstores and distributors worldwide.

For more information on foreign distributors, call 717-532-3040.
Reach us on the Internet: www.destinyimage.com.

ISBN 13 TP: 978-0-7684-7974-4
ISBN 13 eBook: 978-0-7684-7975-1

For Worldwide Distribution, Printed in the U.S.A.
1 2 3 4 5 6 7 8 / 28 27 26 25 24

Contents

A Calm Hour with God

For thus says the Lord God, the Holy One of Israel: "In returning and rest you shall be saved: in quietness and confidence shall be your strength..."

(Isaiah 30:15 NKJV).

When I first abandoned my life to the Lord in 1996, a man of God picked me up early in the morning for a road trip. As I sat there in the passenger seat, he turned to me and said, "Let's pray." I immediately started to rattle off in tongues, progressively getting louder with fervency and focus. I didn't know what else to do. I was mimicking what I had seen others do and thought that's what you do when you pray. Anyone looking at me would have thought I was in agony, making sounds, rocking back and forth in constant motion. This man of God waited patiently for me to finish machine-gunning God with tongues and desperate cries.

When the smoke finally cleared from my assault on God and war initiation with hell, the car became silent. Then with the steering wheel in one hand and his steaming coffee in the other, this man of God said softly, "Jesus, I worship You." He sat quietly and nearly whispered, "I worship You, precious Lamb of God. There is no one like You. I worship You." In an instant, the undeniable presence of the Holy Spirit filled the car, deeply touching my heart.

The experience intrigued me. *How was he able to invoke God's presence with such ease?* I wondered. This man didn't raise his voice or even appeal to God to manifest Himself. He simply looked to Jesus in adoration. I learned an incredibly valuable lesson that day—*adoration is the secret to experiencing the conscious presence of God*. One ounce of adoration moves God more than any amount of effort and striving. This reminds me of something I read that A. B. Simpson, pastor and theologian, said when he saw people raising their voices in prayer, "People who are always yelling at God must live very far away from Him."

Dear reader, to gaze upon God in sweet fixation and loving worship is more valuable to God than any religious or human practice. We must let this settle into our hearts as adoration puts us in our proper place and places Him in His as Lord over all. As South African Christian pastor Andrew Murray wrote, "There's nothing more humble than adoring Jesus."

Prayer must be understood to be the sustained fixation of the soul upon God. We must recognize that the blood that poured out from the flesh of the God-man was to rend the veil over our eyes so that we could have an endless vision of Jesus. That is what prayer is—"*looking unto Jesus*" (Hebrews 12:1-2). This is the reconciliation: *the restoration of God and man in direct fellowship, finding pleasure in each other.* A. W. Tozer wrote in *The Pursuit of God,* "When the eyes of the soul looking out meet the eyes of God looking in, heaven has begun right here on this earth."

True maturity in God is delighting in Him whether we ever receive the answers to our prayers. So many people have no idea that communion with God can be a great delight. I submit to you that not only can prayer be a great delight, but it should be the very source of all our delight. Flemish mystic writer John Ruysbroeck wrote, "For while we please God and God pleases us, then love is practiced and eternal life."[1]

God's desire is to be your greatest desire. His greatest delight is to be all your delight. One of my Bible school professors rephrased part of the Westminster Confession of Faith as, "The chief end of man is to glorify God by finding pleasure in Him."

What we have in the gospel is God Himself. Is there anything or anyone that can be compared with God? The man of prayer realizes this and believes this and experiences this. He runs to God as his refuge, help, and strength as well as his pleasure, joy, and bliss. "One hour with God infinitely excels all the pleasures and delights of this lower world," wrote David Brainerd, minister and missionary. And Robert Murray M'Cheyne, Scottish minister, said, "A calm hour with God is worth a whole lifetime with man."[2]

How wonderfully brilliant of God to make what is most important easiest and our greatest need our greatest delight. Then we can easily find Him as refuge and delightfully find Him to be everything that is needed.

Notes

1. John Ruysbroeck, *The Little Book of Enlightenment,* https://thevalueofsparrows.wordpress.com/2017/10/04/mysticism-john-ruysbroeck-the-little-book-of-enlightenment/; accessed January 17, 2024.
2. Robert Murray M'Cheyne, Andrew Alexander Bonar (1866), *The Life and Remains, Letters, Lectures, and Poems of [the Rev] Robert Murray McCheyne,* p. 157.

Rest: The Realm of Perception

There remains therefore a rest for the people of God. For he who has entered His rest has himself also ceased from his works as God did from His

(Hebrews 4:9-10 NKJV).

There is a rest that isn't mere deep breaths and relaxation, but rather, the relinquishing of our own efforts. It has often been said, "Faith can be spelled R.E.S.T." This rest-trust in God makes perception of Him possible. I once heard an old saint say, "Overstimulation kills the receptivity of the soul." The inverse is true; rest opens our receptivity of Him.

I constantly need to remind myself of this works-dissolving fact: "[I] stand before God as if [I] were Christ, because Christ stood before God as if he were [me]."[1] That is rest.

So often I have fallen into a striving that seeks to break something open, and I fail to enjoy what Jesus has broken open, namely, the veil between us and God (see Hebrews 10:19-20). It does me well to keep before my eyes the old exhortation of Arthur Burt, "Snuggle, don't struggle." A better summary of our bridal union with Christ I cannot find. I am not negating the scriptural truths that we *"run to win," "wrestle against,"* or endure as a *"soldier"* (see 1 Corinthians 9:24; Ephesians 6:12; 2 Timothy 2:3). Each of these have a place in our earthly sojourn, but none of these analogies refer to our experience of the presence of God. They simply cannot be applied to the blissful communion we have with Christ in the gospel. That, my precious reader, is a gift (see Acts 10:45). Not only is it undeserved, it cannot be earned. It is simply received.

Restored fellowship with God is the cream of the goodness of the good news. By faith in Christ, we receive what He deserves, because He bore what we deserved. That is the rest to which I am referring; that quiet trust in Christ is our only means of receiving from God.

That rest granted to us by faith in Christ is why I believe the exhortation, "Snuggle, don't struggle," is the sum of victorious Christianity. Our Christ-wrought access to God ends all struggling and gives us the intimate privilege of snuggling, hidden in His bosom, captured by His charms and enraptured in His arms. If we lay our heads upon His breast, we gain access to the divine treasure chest. In this treasure chest are all the riches of Christ Himself (see Colossians 2:3). The riches of Christ that we receive *"through the knowledge of Him"* are all that we need for *"life and godliness"* (2 Peter 1:3 NKJV). The glorious gospel gives us rest. As the lines of this poem so eloquently attest:

> He came His arm round me;
> I leaned upon His chest;
> I did not long to feel more strong
> So sweet the childlike rest.
>
> —Selected

In the gospel, we are lifted and carried by Him. This rest-trust in Christ is the antithesis of human effort. As F. B. Meyer exhorts us to, in all circumstances of life, "Remind God of His entire responsibility."[2] No man can boast of anything when he realizes that his Christian life is by God's grace through faith in Him. This is not of ourselves. Salvific rest is a ceasing of striving and a casting of oneself upon God's mercy. By faith in the gospel, we quickly realize that our need isn't to be self-strong, but to be still. The former obstructs rather than encourages a life of experiential union with God.

Rest is simply this; the soul giving God His proper place. This rest is brilliantly described in a paragraph from Charles Spurgeon:

> The Puritans speak of faith as a recumbency, a leaning. It needs no power to lean; it is a cessation from our own strength, and allowing our weakness to depend upon another's power. Let no man say, "I cannot lean;" it is not a question of what you can do, but a confession of what you cannot do, and a leaving of the whole matter with Jesus.[3]

Notes

1. "Justification by Faith," *The Spurgeon Archive,* Spurgeon sermon on April 28, 1867, Metropolitan Tabernacle Pulpit, Volume 49; http://www.romans45.org/spurgeon/sermons/3392.htm; accessed January 17, 2024.
2. F. B. Meyer, "Our Daily Homily," *Christian Classics Ethereal Library;* https://ccel.org/ccel/meyer/homily2/homily2.cxlvi.html; accessed January 17, 2024.
3. Charles Haddon Spurgeon, "Laying the Hand on the Sacrifice," Spurgeon sermon, August 12, 1877, Metropolitan Tabernacle Pulpit, Volume 49; https://www.spurgeon.org/resource-library/sermons/laying-the-hand-on-the-sacrifice/#flipbook/; accessed January 17, 2024.

Earnestly I Seek You

You, God, are my God, earnestly I seek you...

(Psalm 63:1 NIV).

A professor of mine in Bible college, Dr. Robert Gladstone, once told us that in "worship is the soul's attempt to quench its thirst." One can worship anything, for we can set our inward gaze upon whatever we wish. This is our individuality, the freedom to choose Him or not, which is the game of love. Oh, how He longs for our love.

Though many profess God in the public place, God is only worshiped and adored truly by those who seek Him in the private place. Our musician, full of the rich, tangible presence of God, says, *"You, God, are my God; earnestly I seek you."* To seek God is to intentionally set our will upon Him. God is only our God when He is our pursuit. To not seek Him is to reject Him as God. To not seek Him is to seek something else. The resolution to set the inward gaze of our soul upon God in earnestness and sober diligence is the only true worship of God. *His presence, His Person, His voice, His Word, and His will are our source of life, objective of life, and joy of life.*

Oh, to keep before us the simple truth that His will is in His presence and His presence is in His will! Such a submission to God is entrance into a glorious experience of God. An experience in which is not only satisfaction but also, at times, rapturous delight that can even overflow in the soul to such degree that the physical body can be effected.

David stated, *"My flesh longs for You."* Have you had such an experience? The bliss of His presence so overwhelming that your physical body feels a sort of heavenly delight? Such wondrous heavenly glories, regardless of the tribulations of life, are our lot. The bliss of drugs, sex, and pleasures in this world that turn men out of their minds are so far inferior to the ecstasy we experience in God. These other things are all counterfeits of the glory of God's Person satisfying the soul through direct contact with Him. Because man doesn't realize that he was made to live united with God through surrender to

Him, he seeks out pleasures for himself outside of God. Herein is the self-life that keeps men bound in misery and emptiness.

Heaven seeps its way into the earth through the lives of those who seem to experience heaven while on the earth. Charles Spurgeon said that Robert Chapman was "the saintliest man [he] ever knew."[1] I believe the reason is found in the words of Robert Chapman's friend John Nelson Darby, "We talk of the heavenliness, but Robert Chapman lives in them."[2] To live a satisfied, peaceful life is a result of experiencing the bliss that God is. Such a life is the representation of the salvation that He offers to the world in Christ.

Anyone can tell me it is raining outside, but a man drenched with water as he walks into a room is dripping with the substance of his testimony. The Christian who lives satisfied with God testifies to the world that God is enough. The Christian who doesn't live satisfied with God testifies to the world that God is not enough.

An old saintly woman was asked, "What is this gospel that you believe, and how do you believe it?" Her reply is rest and joy itself: "God is satisfied with His Son—that is the gospel I believe. I am satisfied with Him, too—that is how I believe it."

Notes

1. Robert C. Chapman, *Hymnary.org;* https://hymnary.org/person/Chapman_RC; accessed January 17, 2024.
2. Ibid.

Always Needing Him

...I thirst for you, my whole being longs for you...
(Psalm 63:1 NIV).

The soul thirsts for God. The word *thirst* is the perfect term to capture both desire and need. God Himself is the soul's greatest need and desire. Those who recognize Him humble themselves and cry, "My soul thirsts for You."

Apart from submission to God's Spirit, the soul is a fountain of wickedness, restive, rebellious, and unmanageable, crying out in desperate thirst for satisfaction. Endless attempts are constantly being made among humanity to excel and attain heights and depths to satisfy what the heart and mind thirst for. And what many fail to realize through their whole sojourning upon the earth is that satisfaction for the soul apart from submission to God is simply not possible.

Relationships and romantic ideas of life are tirelessly pursued in an attempt to quench the burning thirst inside man's affections. But it is simply not possible. David, the man after God's own heart states, *"My soul thirsts for You"* (Psalm 63:1 NKJV). The recognition in his spiritual life is that only the Person of God—namely, His presence and voice—can extinguish the flickering crazed scramble of the soul.

Beloved, we need God. We will always need Him. He is an infinite ocean depth of happy rest. He is the endless wellspring of life, the inexhaustible Source. He is the constant bliss, joy, and peace of being. Without His presence, the soul extends itself toward other things, lesser things, things that can never satisfy; and if they are tolerated, they will inflict great damage.

The Embrace We Long For

And He took them up in His arms, laid His hands on them, and blessed them

(Mark 10:16 NKJV).

Dear reader, because I do not know you personally, I wonder if you have ever taken time to strip everything away and just simply sit with God? If you have, I'm sure you recognized something about Him. All He's interested in doing is holding you close. The Church thrives in no other place.

The sweet, intimate experience of Jesus, the cooling drink of the Spirit is a direct contact with God that satisfies the soul out of itself. A surrendered, yielded, trusting faith experiences the embrace for which our souls are longing. Though such an experience may come through a church meeting, a conference, a betrayal, a sickness, a loss, or a rock-bottom experience, it doesn't have to. It should be the source of our daily joy, life, peace, and strength. Nothing is more authentically transformative as laying everything else aside and simply coming to Him.

When my daughter was young, I saw her crying in her room about something. I was deeply concerned, so I walked into the room and bent down to her level and sweetly asked her, "What is wrong, baby?" She began to tell me her pressing issue. She expounded on her disturbing problem, and I picked her up, laid her head on my chest, and said, "Whenever you feel frustrated, sad, angry, confused, or hurt, or anything, you run straight to Daddy, and I'll put your head on my chest, and you can find rest. Forget about everything else and just know that I am here. I can help you. After you calm down, I can handle whatever it is." She didn't respond with anything but a deep sigh of comfort and quietness as she rested on my chest and I rubbed her back. In that moment, a communication deeper than words took place. There was an *exchange happening*. There was a transferring of my rest into her problem.

Often, we feel that what is happening in our lives is very important or troublesome, and we cry and stress. If we will go straight to Him and simply lay our heads on

His chest, He will be our rest. We will find that He is more important than whatever is pressing upon us.

I am afraid that we have theologically reduced God's embrace of the human soul to a symbol. Could it be that there is lifelessness in the Church today because we have failed to point people to God Himself? Could it be that we have emphasized something more than the real experience of His embrace? Could it be that a large part of our deep depravity in prayer is due to a lack of our souls receiving the embrace of God? Could it be that many Christians have a very difficult time maturing by reason of a lack of touch?

God is never responsible for an inconsistent experience of Him. The fault falls on our unwillingness to fall into His arms. My personal belief is that without the embrace of God in our lives, we are quickly decaying. Charles Spurgeon wrote in the classic devotional *Morning and Evening*, "He kills your doubts and your fears by the closeness of His embrace." Sometimes the greatest thing God can say to us is not intelligible at all, it's simply being held. We may not know what He is saying, but we will sense what He is doing. He values the indelible more than the intelligible.

If we allow the Spirit of God to woo us away from our sins, failures, weaknesses, performance, strivings, troubles, and trials, and into His arms, we will find rest. Living in His rest is both the mark of maturity and the maturing work. We must be willing to see that only He matters. We demonstrate this by leaving everything else behind.

Pray this with me, "Precious God, hold me. Drain out my inward poison. Hold me and cause competition, comparison, lust, greed, anger, offense, and frustration to dissolve in me. Hold me and give me love that I don't have, joy that I long for, peace that I need, self-control, patience, kindness, and all those things that You are."

Yielding into Adoration

Be still, and know that I am God...

(Psalm 46:10 NKJV).

One of the first keys to experiencing intimacy with Jesus is understanding the intimate words in Song of Solomon, *"Let him kiss me"* (Song of Solomon 1:2 NKJV). Yielding is the secret, the ceasing of efforts and our still surrender in adoration. Let us yield to Him with no agenda but to let Him hold us.

Can we be so simple as to trust Him to perform His work as we sit quiet in adoration, casting all helplessly upon Him. Can we yield until our spiritual eyes see the rivers of His refreshing glistening with the light of His countenance? Can we yield to no other end than to be yielded, and remain? This is where the kiss is. Madame

Guyon, one of the leading mystics of the Quietist movement, wrote:

> When you are quiet before God, simply allow yourself time to enjoy His presence and be filled full in your spirit. ...Hearing is a passive rather than an active procedure. Rest. Rest. Rest in God's love. Simply listen and be attentive to God. These passive actions will permit God to communicate His love to you.... When your spirit is centered on God all activities He initiates will be full of peace and natural and so spontaneous that it will appear to you that there has hardly been any activity at all.
>
> —Madame Guyon, *Experiencing the Depths of Jesus Christ*

Often, we cannot hear God or experience His heart simply because our hearts are not willing to yield enough to wait for God. The sad fact is, for many of us, His presence is no longer the purpose of prayer. Waiting is yielding to God by taking the time to give all our attention. It's a *turning* of our attention, if you will. When you turn and sustain your gaze wholeheartedly in adoration upon God, little by little your soul will begin to detach from the cares of this world. It will release your heart from self-consciousness and dissolve the "itch of efforts" and the "frenzy of need."

In giving God all our attention, we become quiet *and* still. *Quietness is the absence of external noise. Stillness is the absence of internal noise.* So many people become quiet in their surroundings but are filled with noise internally; thus, they have no stillness. Our need is not to merely be quiet, but to *be still.* What we really need to hear the Lord is to remove ourselves from the hurricane outside *and* to silence the clatter inside.

At this point, His presence will begin to be sensible. By this I mean a sense of sweet tranquility that moves throughout your being, as a direct result of your soul yielding to the Spirit. Without His presence, we will get tired of waiting, because we must understand that we do not wait *for* His presence, but *in* His presence. We must note that, in these moments of yielding in His presence, the purpose of prayer is being accomplished. Here we resign ourselves to linger, content with Him alone. This is what I wish someone would have told me at the very beginning of my fellowship with God.

Lingering is gazing upon Him by sustaining all our attention upon Him. Soon the clutter clears, and we can hear, perceive, know, or oftentimes find contentment with

Him. The bliss of His presence is found in the enjoyment of waiting upon Him.

When we wait on the Lord, it pulls the Word to us. David said, "*...I wait for Your word*" (Psalm 119:74 NASB). In other words, the *word* comes through *waiting*. If we would take time to simply wait on Him, we would receive His word, experience His heart, and see His speaking through various means, the richest of which is unearthed by meditation upon the Scriptures.

Impatience is often the very thing that steals our attention and doesn't allow us to wait on the Lord. *Impatience is an idol factory*. If we don't want to wait on God, and we decide to go do *something else,* we are putting something else in His place. Remember when Moses went to the mountain and Israel became restless? They fashioned an idol in His place, and they even named the idol "Yahweh" (see Exodus 32:4-5).

You can name your idol whatever you'd like. You can name it something spiritual or positive sounding. It matters not. It is still an object that is wrongfully taking the place of God. It's simple: if the origin is off, the whole thing is off. If we don't want to wait for the operation of God's Spirit, we are left with human effort and ingenuity. Oh, to live prioritizing that Holy Dove that ascended on

Christ who waited and refused to move on without Him. Impatience is disinterest in the Dove.

Oh, the danger of allowing busyness to eliminate the simple tranquility of *waiting*. If we choose not to wait and be still, we are actually saying to the Lord, "I've got this. I don't need You to rule me. I'll go forward saying all the right things and sounding the part, but I don't need Your actual reign in my life." However, when we wait upon Him, we give Him His proper throne in our hearts.

If someone is trying to lead us or communicate to us, our attention is most important. If our attention is not fully given to the leader or communicator by listening, by looking, and by concentration, their attempt to communicate to us will not be received in wholeness because we are divided. Keeping our attention upon God is how we can be led by Him. What we do when God seems silent is the greatest revealer of what really has our affection and our attention.

Our relationship with God hinges upon our attentiveness and wholehearted fixation upon His Person and presence. No matter how subtle it may seem in the moment or how meaningless, it is in our looking and in our listening that we find the very source Himself. The subtle impressions of His presence will increase into ecstatic blissful currents if we refuse to irreverently move past them. I have to remind myself that the precious love exchange with God is often right behind the things I want from Him if I will refuse to let them take my attention away from Him.

This love fountain will numb the soul to unbelief, questions, the itch to do, the craving to be noticed, the lusts of the soul, and even the body's longings. This internal bliss is needed to make us more like Him. Such experiential communion brings us into the experience of our individual union with God that Christ has given to us.

Living a life in intimate communion with God is life's greatest joy, peace, satisfaction, success, and pleasure, whether we preach to millions or change tires.

THE JOY OF ABIDING

The kingdom of God is not eating and drinking, but righteousness and peace and joy in the Holy Spirit

(Romans 14:17 NKJV).

God wants to give you a gift. It's called joy. All you have to do is receive it. Your merit doesn't release it. His goodness does. There are no hoops to jump through or special requirements. Red tape isn't the language of the Kingdom.

I believe the Lord is releasing the gift of joy on the body of Christ because we so desperately need it. We have a serious joy famine on our hands. Many people deal with a real sense of heaviness. They become scattered in their minds. Excess thinking is the norm. This ought not to be.

If there is one thing that I'm seeing in my travels, it's this: the Church is lacking joy. The Bible says joy is in the

Kingdom! And if there is any flow from the Vine to the branch, the fruit that will grow as a result is joy. You can bank on joy when you touch God. God brings His realm with Him when He comes. His nature is joy.

When He is allowed in, He dispenses His Person into you. In this, joy becomes part of you, and it's no longer dependent upon circumstances around you, but upon the God who is in you. In the mode of receiving, your joy can't be touched by anything in the natural, for your joy is rooted in the Vine—in abiding in the Vine.

FOUR KEYS TO AID IN ABIDING

Jesus answered and said to him, "If anyone loves Me, he will keep My word; and My Father will love him, and We will come to him and make Our home with him"

(John 14:23 NKJV).

There are four short keys that I believe will aid us in abiding in His presence, the first of which is *living for His presence.* We must wake up every day and remember that this day has been given to us, above all things, to enjoy our God. No matter what task is standing before us, we must adjust our soul's disposition to see that our first priority is to live for His presence. Christian missionary George Muller wrote, "The first great and primary business to which I ought to attend every day was, to have my soul happy in the Lord."[1]

The second key is to *live in His presence.* We must consciously abide in that inner place where the Spirit's presence is known and experienced. To do this, we must live a collected life. The major attack upon the abiding place is scatteredness. The devil knows that if he can scatter your soul, it will not be *still* enough to plug into the socket of Life. It will remain too self-conscious to become God-conscious. Our job is to simply plug into the wall. God's job is the infusion of power.

Infusion is when the properties of one become useful in another. It is when two different things become one. To live in His presence, we must remain settled in Him by worship and surrender. If at all we feel the scattering of the soul, we must turn within by worship and surrender till the soul is stilled and plugged into the infusion of His Spirit in our spirit—the residence of divine glory. Madame Guyon said, "When at any time the passions are turbulent, a gentle retreat inwards unto a Present God, easily deadens and pacifies them; and any other way of contending with them rather irritates than appeases them."[2]

The third key is to *live around His presence.* I suggest this to mean that we make every decision of our lives, moments, and days around the fact that we are living for, in, and by His presence. How many things that are eating our lives away on a daily basis would be set to the side if we looked at every decision in life from the desire to maximize our reception of God? This may strike you as a bit merciless, but it drives the point home with one hard wallop. American revivalist preacher, Jonathan Edwards resolved to "never to do anything, which I would be afraid to do, if it were the last hour of my life."[3]

The fourth key is to *live from His presence*. Our counsel, words, preaching, life, and presence will carry life if they issue from a life that is living in the presence of God. We must remain in His presence, consciously and experientially, and allow everything that we are to flow from that river within. If we make Him our fountain, then He shall flow through every stream.

Because of God's call upon my life to bring the Church into a deeper experience with the Life of God, I am constantly criticized as a "sunshine and rainbows" preacher. I have had ministers who are older, wiser, and more constant in the faith than myself come up to me and say, "There is coming a day when God will leave you to yourself and the enemy, and there you will find out what you are truly made of." One older saint said to my father when they saw the burning love the Spirit poured out in my soul at the beginning, "He will come down with the rest of us after a while." Perhaps they are right. At the time of this writing, I am thirty years in the Lord, and maybe I am too young and naïve to understand "abandonment" time. But all I know and preach is that He prepares *"a table before me in the presence of my enemies"* (Psalm 23:5).

No matter what surrounds me, I can have sweet communion with Him. If He had to leave me to test me, then that would mean that He is seeking to fashion me into something apart from Himself. If the gospel is that He would afterwards abandon me to see if I can make it on the power of human resolve apart from dependency on Him, apart from His empowering presence, then it is not a gospel of union with God.

I heard an old saint preach that, if a Christian cannot find comfort in God in his darkest hour, then the gospel and the Spirit are a farce. I don't buy it. I need Him and the sweet meals He prepares for me right in front of an enormous army of devils salivating for my soul.

He has *"anointed my head with oil,"* smearing His own substance upon me (Psalm 23:5 NASB). The dripping of His oil and the fragrance of His ointment are continually upon us. Notice that *the anointing follows the table*; we eat of Him, receiving Him internally, and then He rests upon us externally. I once heard an amazing man of God say that the presence of the Lord is internal while the anointing of the Lord is external. David expounded upon this with the next statement, *"My cup runs over"* (Psalm 23:5 NKJV). When the presence of the Lord fills the inner man, it will begin to spill over and onto the outer man, just like a cup that is being filled when it overflows the sides and covers the outside. This Shepherd is so good! He lets us rest, drink, wash, eat, and then He overflows in us. The inflow creates overflow, which creates an outflow.

Notes

1. "The First Great and Primary Business," *GeorgeMuller.org;* https://www.georgemuller.org/devotional/the-first-great-and-primary-business; accessed January 17, 2024.
2. Madam Guyon, "Short and Easy Method of Prayer," *Christian Classics Ethereal Library;* https://ccel.org/ccel/guyon/prayer/prayer.xiii.html?highlight=When%20at%20any%20time%20the%20passions%20are%20turbulent&queryID=31705162&resultID=130280#highlight; accessed January 17, 2024.
3. Jonathan Edwards, "The Resolutions of Jonathan Edwards," DesiringGod; https://www.desiringgod.org/articles/the-resolutions-of-jonathan-edwards; accessed January 17, 2024.

"Do You Want to Know the Secret?"

But you, when you pray, go into your room, and when you have shut your door, pray to your Father who is in the secret place; and your Father who sees in secret will reward you openly

(Matthew 6:6 NKJV).

Recently, I had a dream. A very special person whom I highly respect as a man of God came to me in the dream and said, "Hey, do you want to know the secret of union with God?"

I said, "Yeah, I do."

Then he grabbed me and pulled me into a room away from everybody else. He shut the door. I leaned in to hear these amazing words of wisdom that would reveal to me the secret.

He then simply opened his mouth and softly and intimately sang, "Jesus, I love You. Jesus, I love You. Jesus, I love You." He completely forgot about me. He even forgot about himself. He continued, "Jesus, I love You."

When I woke from the dream, I thought to myself, *You know, he never told me the special secret.* Then I realized he was exemplifying the secret for me, which is:

1. Get away from people.
2. Shut the door.
3. Forget yourself.
4. Forget everyone else.
5. Lift your heart in tender love to Christ.

That's the secret. It is tragic to admit, but I feel that, sometimes, we want something more than that. Yet there just isn't anything more than to love Him. Because *in loving Him, we receive Him.* He is everything. The eternal object of love.

DWELLING IN HIS SHADOW

Now the Lord appeared to Abraham by the oaks of Mamre, while he was sitting at the tent door in the heat of the day

(Genesis 18:1 NASB).

The Lord appeared to Abraham *"while he was sitting."* Abraham was not running, standing, leaning, or even sleeping. Abraham was sitting, consciously resting, still and alone. Don't let this slip by unnoted: Abraham was still, at rest, and alone.

Where exactly was he sitting? *"At the tent door."* What is the significance of the tent? Well, do you recall that Abraham had been called out from his home to enter a land that he did not know? He had torn his heart from his homeland and family to obey the voice of God. His life is the testimony and model of our earthly sojourning as aliens and strangers in this earth (see 1 Peter 2:11).

The tent is a statement, declaring that this world was not his home and that, despite an earthly Promised Land, he waited for something from heaven (see Hebrews 11:10,14-16). Abraham refused to sink his feet into the soil of this earth simply because of the word that the Lord had spoken to him.

Under this tent, Abraham was resting in the shade from *"the heat of the day."* What a wonderful picture: Abraham rested under the shadow. Doesn't that same picture find its home in the lover of Song of Solomon 2:3 (NKJV), *"I sat down in his shade with great delight,"* or the psalmist in Psalm 63:7 (NKJV), *"in the shadow of Your wings I will rejoice."* Abraham was resting, quiet, and delighting in the shade of the Most High.

Friend, this is where the encounter realm is found—resting in His sweetness and hiding beneath His great love that obstructs the inevitable heat of life. Before we can understand why Abraham's friendship with God brought him into contact with the heart of God, we must understand the spiritual life that Abraham lived with God: he rested under the shadow of the Almighty; he dwelt in this place of shade; he stayed in the refuge of God.

The ground for life-defining encounters with God's glory is the daily experience of His glorious shadow.

Opening the Eyes by Adoration

Unto You I lift up my eyes, O You who dwell in the heavens (Psalm 123:1 NKJV).

In the midst of the heat of life, under the shadow at the door of his tent, Abraham *lifted up his eyes.* The lifting of the eyes to the Lord is a picture of worship because we choose to fix our attention above the earthly cares of life and ascend to God, moving beyond the horizontal plane into the vertical. Abraham was able to look unto God without hesitation and reservation because he had already left everything for Him.

This faithful old man, having already proved God's faithfulness, neither strived nor strained, but simply looked up from his place of rest in the shade. Here, in adoration, he saw. Friend, this is also where you will see—*as you adore Jesus, you will see Him.*

Abraham lifted his eyes above the world unto God and looked with his eyes, giving his attention to God's presence. And he saw three persons. Though two of these were angels, it is interesting to note that three appeared to him. How utterly perfect this symbolism is: the vision is a triune vision. The vision of God is always threefold, revealing the Father by the Son and the Son through the Spirit.

Being God's Resting Place

My Lord, if I have now found favor in Your sight, do not pass on by Your servant. Please let a little water be brought, and wash your feet, and rest yourselves under the tree
(Genesis 18:3-4 NKJV).

It is wonderful to note that these three persons stand opposite Abraham. The vision of God is always completely opposite to what we are. Every time we truly see Him, we should be utterly convicted of how much we are not like Him, for He is holy and altogether separate from all things. He is other than us at every point, and our vision of Him will always reveal the same.

Abraham had a vision of three persons opposite to where he was, and his vision of them infused him with a great need to run to them. Gripped with desire, Abraham must respond. For us, all God has to do is reveal Himself, and the magnetic attraction of His nature and Person causes us to leave everything else behind. (I can hear the Lover sing, "Draw Me and I will run after you.") Running to Him is a lover's action.

Notice that Abraham didn't run up to the visitors and start shaking their hands as if he were like them; rather, he threw himself to the ground in worship. Worship always produces worship. Adoration always plunges you deeper into adoration. Abraham was humbled in adoration, low at the feet of these three.

I asked my friend Andrew Lamb, pastor of Acts 2 Church in Orlando, Florida, "If Jesus were to show up in your room one morning in prayer, what would you say to Him?"

His response was amazing: "Don't leave!"

Abraham said something similar: "Lord, if I have found favor in Your sight, please do not pass Your servant by." God had come to visit him, and Abraham begged Him to stay.

Notice that Abraham addressed God as Lord. The kind of individual who has rich communion experiences with God is the one who submits to God as Lord. In Luke 6:46 (NKJV) Jesus said, *"Why do you call Me 'Lord, Lord,' and do not do the things which I say?"* Today, many profess God as their Lord because they know that is what He is supposed to be, but they refuse to submit to Him. Abraham was not this way. He acknowledged God as his Lord because he had already left everything in response to hearing God's voice.

Abraham also called himself the Lord's servant. A servant is someone who lives to meet the needs of another. Abraham lived to meet God's needs; he had left all. He lifted up his eyes, he looked to see God, he lay before the Lord, and he immediately longed to serve Him and sought to be God's resting place: "Please let me wash Your feet. Please rest under the tree." I wonder if this wasn't what Jesus referenced when He said that the Father, the Son, and the Spirit would make their abode in us: "*Jesus answered and said to him, 'If anyone loves Me, he will keep My word; and My Father will love him, and We will come to him and make Our home with him'*" (John 14:23 NKJV).

Staying Within the Cloud

So Moses went into the midst of the cloud...

(Exodus 24:18 NKJV).

Once, I was in an airport in Seattle, and as I was waiting for my plane to arrive, I observed a plane just after takeoff enter into a cloud. It was absorbed up into the cloud, and the sight of the plane was no more. Such is the swallowing of the life of the believer in the substance of God. The two distinctly different elements become nearly indistinguishable. The lesser is swallowed by the greater. It is difficult to tell where one ends and the other begins.

For the one who seeks union with God, it is simply not enough to merely be around the cloud; there is a burning fire within that one to go into the cloud. Multitudes stand outside and are content there. But the desperate lover wants to enter the cloud Himself. This lover is convinced and convicted of his deep need of the voice of God. As the psalmist said, *"He spoke to them in the cloudy pillar"* (Psalm 99:7 NKJV). God did release His voice from the cloud and around the cloud, but the speaking that is in the cloud is a completely different kind of speaking. The presence around the cloud is wonderful, but it can be penetrated. The experience of His presence is deep, but it can be plunged deeper. His exhilarating voice is reserved for the one who will go in, not satisfied with merely being around His presence, but burning to be absorbed by Him.

Madame Guyon in her commentary on Exodus wrote, "It is the property of God's speaking to absorb our own." God is calling us into the cloud to release His speaking into us—not just to inform us of His desires or educate us in a message, but rather to make us His voice by swallowing us in His own substance. Not just receiving His speaking, but *becoming His speaking.* Notice the lives of the prophets. They became the oracle, the burden. The actual speaking of the prophet issued out of what the prophet was.

When John the Baptist was asked who he was, he responded, *"I am 'The voice of one crying in the wilderness...'"* (John 1:23 NKJV). He was God's means of communication to the world. This is what God is after. This is a prophetic generation, a people swallowed by God's own substance.

As we penetrate the presence and the presence penetrates us, His holiness and purity permeate us. The inevitable work of God's nearness is Godlikeness. He is Truth and true thoroughly. As the light of His presence exposes our sin, we cast ourselves deeper upon and into Him—He who alone makes men holy (see Psalm 90:8). The presence of God has this incredible dichotomous work to it. He will make us holy in His very own presence. *His presence is the workshop of holiness.*

The Whisper of the Bridegroom

I charge you, O daughters of Jerusalem, if you find my beloved, that you tell him I am lovesick!

(Song of Solomon 5:8 NKJV)

My prayer is that you find a "secret unction" hidden under these words that will compel you to taste and enjoy the Bridegroom in a way far beyond your wildest imagination of holy romance. As God's ultimate desire is to dispense His own Life into His creatures through *communing* with the words of His heart, I am convinced that God will lavish His perfect love upon you through this unlearned and foolish heart of mine.

In recent weeks, my heart felt that "holy itch" to write again, but I had no idea what He wanted me to write; so, I waited. Oh, precious one, did you notice that last sentence? Waiting is the divine sifting in which God can remove the dross-filled desire for attention, significance, and the terrible plague of human reasoning that offers to God things that are so contrary to His nature that He cannot, and never will, accept them. Waiting pulls the whisper of the Bridegroom toward the ear of our soul.

Something in the deepest part of me is crying out! *The Holy Spirit is trying His best to introduce the body of Christ to the Living Bridegroom.* But it seems to me that our hearts are set on everything else but Him. You see it is not about falling on the floor. It is not about preaching. It is not about evangelizing. It is not about pastoring. It is not about buildings. It is not about money. *It is about the Lord Jesus Christ.*

I can hear John Kilpatrick, who had pastoral oversight of the historic Brownsville Revival, saying in my heart to Jesus, "I want You. I don't want religion. I don't want another church. I don't want another congregation. I don't want another Bible. I don't want another wife. I don't want more kids. I want You, Lord!"

Dear reader, we must have Jesus. Jesus alone! His presence! Just Him. Only Him. *Precious Bridegroom, captivate our hearts again!*

As I waited for a few months before writing a word, pushing away the urge simply to fill a page with truths and clever articulations, God met me in a wonderful way. This life-changing personal experience is what has birthed these pages. You might ask, "What does your personal experience have to do with my life?" I know that God's nature is to take the words herein that He has spoken into me, and the experiences that He has thrust upon me, to pull you into a greater, more profound experience of His Son.

Whether you are thriving in God or barely surviving in God, this lovesick treatise will aid the health of your soul. To borrow the words of A. W. Tozer, "...but if my fire is not large it is yet real, and there may be those who can light their candle at its flame."[1]

Pray this with me. "Precious Living Bridegroom, make Yourself audible to my heart, tangible to my spirit and visible to my soul that I may love You more than I do now."

NOTE

1. A. W. Tozer, *The Pursuit of God* (Chicago, 1948).

His Starry-Eyed Bride

I am my beloved's, and his desire is toward me
(Song of Solomon 7:10 NKJV).

Many search their entire lives for such a union. "Soulmate," as it is called, is just another term expressing the deep desire of humanity to be fulfilled. We who have laid our hearts at the feet of Christ know a satisfaction far more delightful than mere human union.

For God has become a Man yet still remained God. Jesus is the holy name of that unfathomable merger. And with Him, we have the fullest union and most delightful experience of complacent love.

The bride in Song of Solomon spoke of being her lover's current possession. *"I am my beloved's,"* free from the restless anticipation of "maybe someday" or the wearying uncertainty of performing to obtain Him as a reward; she was then His.

She was settled. No more racing. No more chasing. She could rest in His arms. Fully His. Accepted. *"I am my beloved's."* She was not her own. Her desires were not for herself anymore. She saw her future was His. Her passions were His. Her mind and will were His. She was gladly owned. If such a thought was not sufficient to bring joy unspeakable into the soul, she spoke further: *"His desire is for me."*

We know what it is to desire something. God has installed in us such a capability. We have all sought ways to obtain things we want. We have arranged life in certain ways to obtain certain ends. We have put ourselves "through the mill" at times, moved by such a force as desire. God has installed this. He did so seeking to explain how He feels toward us. For having installed desire and made its deep feeling known to us in everyday life, He writes, *"I have loved you with an everlasting love"* (Jeremiah 31:3 NKJV). He desires us.

Jesus has suffered Himself in order to seek us out and win our love. And that is all. The Bridegroom did not mention His desire for something from her. She knew His desire was for her. For her person. Not for her services.

Not for her land or money or heritage or help. He had looked at her in such a way. Her blushing face said, "He wants me." No doubts or additions. He desired her. He was all-in for her. None other has desired you so much.

To be desired by someone is wonderful; and God Himself is far more than our minds could ever grasp. Millennia upon millennia will expound upon such a truth to our hearts. Even angels ask, *"What is man that You are mindful of him?"* (Psalm 8:4 NKJV).

Reader, you are loved. Don't allow anyone to dissuade you from security in His arms. Refuse to listen to anything not fragrant with His desire for you. Daily set your heart higher than the world and all other loves by saying, "I am my Beloved's, and His desire is for me."

Neglecting the Bridegroom

The watchmen who make the rounds in the city found me, they struck me and wounded me; the guards of the walls took my shawl away from me

(Song of Solomon 5:7 NASB).

Have you ever felt the effects of neglect? Madame Guyon wrote in her journal, "By neglect I have been pillaged." To be pillaged is to be overtaken and robbed unnecessarily. We find that when we neglect the Lord, we get into all sorts of unnecessaries. The bride was struck and wounded with unnecessary scars. Her shawl was also taken. Neglect brings unnecessary losses. The bride then realized in neglect that her safety was in the beloved's person.

I feel as though the Lord looks at many of His people and asks, "Did you marry Me, or did you marry him? Did you marry Me, or did you marry that?" It doesn't matter what "it" is. It could be a person or a pursuit, yet if it has more of your attention than Jesus, it will negatively affect everything.

Is not our lack of peace and joy an indication that our love is somewhere compromised? Perhaps a person in your life has more of your attention than Christ. Let me ask you, did that person die for you? Maybe an interest has risen up and captivated your heart more than Christ. Did that interest rise from the dead? Most certainly not. Yet your Bridegroom bled, died, and rose to win first place in your heart.

We should never let a day go by that we do not drink deeply of Him. The holy Bridegroom has given His limitless Self as an installed well of Living Water. There is no reason to be dry—you have God inside. The bride should be the most satisfied person the world has ever seen because she has the Bridegroom. In essence, Jesus said to the woman at the well in John 4:5-24 (NKJV): "*Go, call your husband and come back.*" She responded, "*I have no husband.*"

And Jesus said, "That is your problem."

You may say, "I have all of these problems in my life." Your problem is that you do not have a husband. You need to marry Jesus. The woman had five husbands. That is indicative of searching the world for something that only Jesus can be. Only Jesus can satisfy the soul.

That is Bridegroom Living-Water Christianity. He will lift you above earth and wrap you in His bliss.

The Jealousy of the Bridegroom

Set me as a seal upon your heart, as a seal upon your arm; for love is strong as death, jealousy as cruel as the grave; its flames are flames of fire, a most vehement flame

(Song of Solomon 8:6 NKJV).

The jealousy of the Bridegroom burns like a flame and flashes like fire. Do you remember when you were first born again and you were so deeply in love with God and nothing would challenge Him? In fact, you were offended when someone suggested that they could take God's place in any way. Nothing would keep you from spending time with Him. You saw everything that stood between you and your prayer closet as a devil from hell. I'm telling you such a love shapes your value system.

Do you remember when hours felt like minutes? Do you remember when the entire Bible seemed to breathe? Do you remember when the sound of worship caused an eruption inside you? The mere thought of being able to worship together with people was sheer joy. Do you remember when there was such an ease in His presence? There were difficulties and tribulations around, no doubt, but for some reason you just soared above them. These were the heights of first love.

Do you remember the sensitivity to the Spirit in the beginning? Do you remember the internal ache in your heart for God? Do you remember making meals for your family and weeping while you did? Washing dishes with dish soap and tears? Do you remember having to pull over while you drove to cry before the Lord?

God remembers these things. He longs for your return. He tells His people throughout Scripture, "Remember!" His message is the same today. First love is what makes the heart of God so happy because in it He gets exactly what He wants, which is to captivate your heart. His goal was never to corner men and collect their consent, but to captivate men's hearts.

Many want to take repentance out of the gospel, yet Jesus says, "Repent," to those who are saved. When you take repentance out of your life, you burn the bridge that leads back to first love.

See, the eyes of the One whom you love masters you. To live in the index of His eyes is first love. The secret to overcoming is being overcome by Him.

"Tell me you're in the ocean, and I'll walk into the sea; raise the waves of Your love, and I'll let them bury me."

Simeon, a Listening Life

And behold, there was a man in Jerusalem whose name was Simeon, and this man was just and devout, waiting for the Consolation of Israel, and the Holy Spirit was upon him
(Luke 2:25 NKJV).

Simeon means "listening" or "to listen." If you think about what listening is in its most basic understanding, it is simply *attentiveness.* And if you think about what attentiveness is, it is the exclusion of all other things except the thing that you are focusing on.

So, *Simeon* means giving God all your attention at the exclusion of all other things. It's living a life of listening. Simeon lived his entire life waiting for the coming of the Lord. It is this waiting, listening, and the exclusion of all other things that is the heart of what I want to continue to emphasize.

The Scriptures say specifically that Simeon was *waiting*. But it says first that the Holy Spirit was *upon him*. Second, it was *revealed to him* by the Holy Spirit that he would not see death before he had seen the Lord's Christ, and third that he *came in the Spirit* to the temple.

There are three things that will accompany a life that listens to the Lord and is literally attentive to Him at the exclusion of all others:

The Holy Spirit will rest upon your life.

The Holy Spirit will reveal. You'll have revelation from the Spirit, spiritual thoughts, spiritual words, spiritual unveilings that lead to the revelation or are the revelation of Jesus.

Your life will be quickened and moved by the Spirit.

The Holy Spirit resting on your life, the revelation that comes from the Holy Spirit, and the Holy Spirit's movement or empowerment, all come from listening. When living a life that gives God all your attention, the Holy Spirit can rest upon you, move you, and reveal Jesus to you.

I believe *Simeon* is what God wants to say to you right now. And I pray that God would grant you grace to listen, to live listening, attentive to His sweet presence. And as you're attentive to His presence, in the midst of even the mundane and all the busyness of life, living listening is living in attentiveness to God.

Many times, it is the addition of other things in our hearts that cause the entrance of fear, anxiety, competition, comparison, and condemnation. All these things that come into the human soul and make a man have to fight and wrestle on the inside are normally leaked in through *inattentiveness.*

I want to encourage you that *listening* is what God is after. This is what will help you. It will place the direct contact of the Spirit upon you. I love the word *upon* because it suggests *underneath.* It suggests that something or someone is over you. It is subjection to God's presence. We cannot claim to be subject to God's presence if our hearts are not attentive to His Person. We are attentive to the Person of God in being attentive to His presence. And we are attentive to the Presence in being attentive to His Person.

So I encourage you that this is yours; it is the new covenant. No matter what's in front of you, no matter what life situation you are in, you can live listening.

The Sound of His Voice

...His voice was like the sound of many waters
(Revelation 1:15 NASB).

Did you know the voice of many waters in Revelation has to do with peace being communicated to you? As a matter of fact, Pennsylvania State University (PSU) studied the effects of sounds on the human brain, and in their findings, they realized that the human brain files sounds away into two different categories: threatening or non-threatening. You have sounds that are threatening, causing an alarm inside, and then you have sounds that are non-threatening to you. Included in the sounds that are non-threatening is the sound of running water, flowing water, or the sound of water itself. The researcher wrote that the sound of water on the human brain is not merely non-threatening, but it's actually calming. The professor of biobehavioral health at PSU even went on to say about flowing water sounds, "It's like they're saying, *'Don't worry, don't worry, don't worry.'*"[1]

I share that to say, when we hear the sweet sound of God's voice, it dispels doubts, fear, and unbelief. He brings in the sweet quiet of His own Person. Inside His voice is such a peace and freedom from the restless worries and the anxieties of life, for His voice is like many waters. He quiets the heart with His love. He comes in and causes the peace that passes all understanding to spread throughout your whole being. Such peace is not only a wonderful experience to live under, but it also is told to us to guard our hearts and minds (see Philippians 4:7).

There is a story about several men working in an icehouse. Before modern refrigeration, there were barns where they stored ice and covered it with hay, keeping the room cool to serve as a refrigerator to preserve foods. Several men were working in this particular icehouse, and while they were working, one of the men lost his watch. When they came out of the barn from working all day, the man said, "Oh, I lost my watch in there." So all the men went into the barn, and they rummaged through all the hay and moved the ice to look for the man's watch. All their efforts proved to be fruitless.

When they came out, the man was saying, "I can't believe I lost my watch." A little boy standing nearby heard that he couldn't find his watch and that he had lost it inside the barn. So, he went into the barn and within ten minutes, came back with the watch. When he returned the watch, the man looked at the boy and said, "How in the world did you find this? We all rummaged through the hay, we moved the ice, and we searched every piece of straw. How did you find my watch?"

The little boy said, "Well, I went into the barn, and I shut the door, and then I lay still and quiet until I heard the ticking of the watch."

I share that to say, for many people, their prayer life is rummaging through the straw, moving the ice, trying to gather many people together to try to affect some sort of encounter with God. But here is the truth: if you will go into the closet and shut the door and silence your heart before Him so that He has all your attention, you will hear the sweet ticking and find the great treasure, the lost treasure, of the Person of Jesus. You will find the riches of the Lord right there in the secret place within.

I encourage you to take some time today to be like that little boy with the watch. Go into a room and be quiet. Lay your head upon His chest and lift your heart up to Him.

Let Him know how much you love Him and receive His love for you. Your heart will begin to open, and then as you open the Scriptures, they will open your spirit even more.

There are three openings: 1) you open your heart to Him, 2) He opens you up, and then 3) the Scriptures open more for you to receive more of Him. The three realms: 1) I open one, which is my heart, and then 2) His love opens another, which causes 3) the Scriptures to open me to His Person. Open to open to open to receive revelation upon revelation upon revelation of His Person.

NOTE

1. Adam Hadhazy, "Why does the Sound of Water Help You Sleep?" *LiveScience.com*, January 18, 2016; https://www.livescience.com/53403-why-sound-of-water-helps-you-sleep.html; accessed January 17, 2024.

"She Loved Me"

Assuredly, I say to you, wherever this gospel is preached in the whole world, what this woman has done will also be told as a memorial to her

(Matthew 26:13 NKJV).

Here was a woman who had poured out her *"costly fragrant oil"* from *"an alabaster flask"* upon the head of Jesus (Matthew 26:7 NKJV). Her name was Mary of Bethany, and Jesus wanted her to be *remembered.* Because that's true, she must be significant! Not only that, He tied the memory of her to the global spread of the gospel.

At first this bothered me, because I thought to myself, She never preached a message. She never taught a class. She never wrote a book. She never performed any miracles. She is only mentioned three times in Scripture. I said, "Lord, what could it be in this woman that would cause her to be tied to the testimony of Your name for all time? What is it that's so special to You?"

As I waited, I heard His voice. He said, *"She loved Me."* It doesn't sound significant, does it? I thought, *"Lord, so many people have loved You! What makes her different?* I realized that God took me to this passage to show me the *kind of love* that she had, which separated her from so many others. The kind of love that she had was intrinsic to the spread of the gospel.

Seated at His Feet

Now it happened as they went that He entered a certain village; and a certain woman named Martha welcomed Him into her house. And she had a sister called Mary, who also sat at Jesus' feet and heard His word

(Luke 10:38-39 NKJV).

The first mention of this woman describes her as sitting at His feet, listening to His words. Isn't that beautiful? Think of this picture: a crowded house full of commotion, and then there was this woman. She was on her knees, and with fixed eyes, she was steadily staring at Him. If I had been there, I would have been struck by her magnificent obsession. It would have hit me hard. Why? Because she didn't care what anyone thought of her. She was looking at

Him. This is the life I want! To gaze upon the Lamb who was slain.

Mary teaches us something very significant. She teaches us that He is too beautiful to look away from. She teaches us that there is actually honey dripping from His lips (see Proverbs 24:14 NIV). The honey that drips from His lips is sweet to our taste! Consistent with this, the psalmist said, *"How sweet are Your words to my taste, sweeter than honey to my mouth!"* (Psalm 119:103 NKJV).

With the mouth men can describe honey, but only the mouth of Jesus dispenses honey. The difference is that teaching and theology will always be inferior to tasting. Proverbs also states, *"My Son, eat honey, for it is good, and the honeycomb which is sweet to your taste; so shall the knowledge of wisdom be to your soul..."* (Proverbs 24:13-14 NKJV).

I see that the story of Mary of Bethany is a call to be captivated by Him! She is a demonstration of His worth. She is a proclamation of the preeminence of His Person. Her love cries out, *"He is greater than His gifts! He is more wonderful than His wonders! Stare at Him for He is greater than the anointing. He is lovely!"* She wasn't standing in awe of His powers. She had found something so much more valuable. She found that He Himself was the fulfillment of her soul, the satisfaction and joy of her life. She was struck breathless by the overwhelming conviction that He is more lovely than anything she had seen.

Mary of Bethany realized that being with Him was to have everything she had ever wanted, it was to be everything she had ever wanted to be, and it was to arrive everywhere she had ever dreamed of going. She found that His presence freed her from the need to have anything else. Most of all, she found that her prayers had vanished simply by His presence.

How? Because she found that He was and is everything she needed and everything she ever wanted. His presence transformed the mundane and common house that she lived in into a garden of spices with her Beloved. She drew near, near enough to hear, if nothing else, His breathing.

One Thing Is Necessary

But one thing is needed, and Mary has chosen that good part, which will not be taken away from her

(Luke 10:42 NKJV).

You might think, "I don't know this life." Let me tell you, Jesus described this life as *"the good part."* He went on to describe it as untouchable and eternal! Following that, He said it is the *"one thing is needed."* In other words, "The only necessity in life is right here, looking at Me."

Mary shows us that the essential Christian message is not to behave, but to *behold*. You can tell who doesn't really want God to rule their lives by who doesn't take time to simply sit and listen to Him.

I wake up at times and put my head on the headboard and just say, "Lord, I have to see You. I have to see You.

I worship You. I must see You." The sweetness of God begins to flow in as the receptivity of my soul begins to open through adoration. He flows in with peace that passes all understanding. He fills my heart with joy unspeakable and full of glory. I tell you, these things are for us! In this, all the situations in our lives have no bearing on whether or not we have peace and joy. Why? Because we are mesmerized and fixed on His Person! This is what Mary was trying to show us.

The Barrenness of a Busy Life

But Martha was distracted with much serving. And she approached Him and said, "Lord, do You not care that my sister has left me to serve alone? Therefore tell her to help me"

(Luke 10:40 NKJV).

Martha was too busy for the bliss and enjoyment of life with Jesus. Her relationship with Jesus was so wrapped up in what she was doing for Him. Oh how easy it is to hide behind activity! Jesus contrasted these two sharply. One sister was looking at Him; the other was not. One sister was listening to Him; the other was not. One sister is near Him; the other was not. One sister was at rest; the other was not. Martha was simply too active to give Him her attention. The Greek philosopher Socrates said, "Beware the barrenness of a busy life."

Martha Kilpatrick writes in her book *Adoration: Mary of Bethany*, "Activity can mask an empty soul and give a fake costume of nobility." Martha chose occupation for the Lord over preoccupation with the Lord. She wanted to feed Him, more than feed on Him. She preferred to be around Him, more than look at Him. So many have become fixated on what is around Him rather than being fixated on looking upon Him! It's a trap to get us to become mesmerized by His ways rather than His Person.

It's so easy to love the flow and forget His face. Oh but there is a face that can always be looked at! As we continue to look at His face, we become blinded to the things that are constantly pulling on us. This is called *satisfaction*. Satisfaction is not a perk of His presence. Satisfaction is the very means by which He frees you and empowers you to be able to obey Him.

Martha was unable to see the real significance of having the Lord in her house. That is exactly what activity can do. It will rob you of your attraction to God. Martha chose to value other things rather than look into His eyes. Martha was fruitless in this scene. The Spirit of God thought that her work was so insignificant that it wasn't even named specifically in the Scriptures. Her work died with her. Yet Mary became a message to all generations connected to the gospel itself. Do you see now?

You say, "What do I do, Eric? Quit my job and move to a cave? I have twelve kids, I'm in school, and I'm running two businesses." Allow me to define busyness to you. Busyness is not having a lot to do. Here is the definition of barren busyness: *to eclipse His worth with work.* It is replacing the simplicity of Christ with the multiplicity of your own ways.

Busyness is not having a lot to do. Jesus had a lot to do, yet it never made its way into Him. He remained disconnected from busyness inwardly to remain connected with His heavenly Father amid everything. In this, His Father became the Source of everything. *Only if He is the center of our life can He be Source.* If He is not the center, He is not Source, and if He is not Source, something else is. That was Martha's problem.

What is dead activity? It's covering the restless, bankrupt state of your soul with things to do, things that God didn't commission. It's easy to keep outward things going while neglecting the simple act of staring into His face.

Isn't it funny that Martha tried to diminish what Mary was doing? But notice that Mary, just like the Lamb she was beholding, offered no rebuttal! Workers always try to murder worshipers in one way or another, but to gaze at Him exposes the ones who are not gazing. This shows me that Mary scandalizes all those who love the work of the Lord more than the Lord of the work. It shows me that the purity of only wanting Him exposes the impurity of merely wanting something from Him.

This choice is ever and always before you and me. We are today what we chose yesterday. We are not today what we neglected yesterday. We will be tomorrow what we elect today. The choice is *yours*. He has made His face completely and totally available.

The One for Whom Jesus Looks

...she...called Mary her sister, saying, "The Teacher has come and is calling for you." As soon as she heard that, she arose quickly and came to Him. ...Then, when Mary came where Jesus was, and saw Him, she fell down at His feet...

(John 11:28-29,32 NKJV).

Mary's brother had died. Then the Lord arrived at the scene, and Martha actually met Him. What did she meet Him with? She talked to Him and gave Him dialogue. Her dialogue was even theological, talking about resurrection and so forth. However, in Christ's dialogue with Martha, He didn't find what He was looking for. So, the Scripture says, *"He looked for Mary"* (John 11:17-28).

Words will never replace worship. He wasn't looking for someone who would throw words at Him. He wanted worship rather than words. He went looking for Mary! The first time I read this, it pierced me deeply. He sought a worshiper. He still does! He is looking for a "Mary" in the middle of a room. He is looking, not for mere words, but for worship in the middle of every meeting.

So, here in the story, Mary came to Jesus. Her brother had died. Her heart was hurting, and she didn't understand. What did she do? She threw herself at His feet. Can you see why she was so special to Him? Everyone else was standing up and talking. They had opinions about this and that, and plenty of unanswered questions. Yet what did Mary do? She threw everything and herself at His feet. An act that professed, "You, Lord, are more lovely and worthy to me than all the answers and facts that I could find!"

Here is the problem: men would rather explain than adore. They would rather inquire than simply adore. Mary shows us that she was willing to worship Him despite not understanding. Certainly, she had feelings and thoughts and questions about the situation—yet she was willing to throw them down, along with her own life, at the feet of Jesus. She was literally saying that *Christ's presence is more important than answers.*

I don't know what you're going through or what you've been through, but I know that He Himself is better than any answer He could give you. Too often, we get distracted by what He gives, and we begin to come to Him for something other than Him. Then we wonder why we keep missing the sweet, blissful enjoyment of His Person.

Even though Mary and Martha had similar discussions with Jesus, He responded with resurrection power to Mary only. Do you see this? Mary shows us that *she would rather move Him than understand Him.* She was more interested in touching Him than defining Him. She shows us that something takes place in adoration that makes understanding not that important anymore. The memory of Mary, which is intrinsic to the gospel, is God's invitation for all to love Him as she loved Him. She is the embodiment of the first commandment.

Mary was mesmerized. In fact, she had symptoms of lovesickness. The primary symptom is a fixed gaze that cannot look away or be broken. I pray that you would become so lovesick that you would have this same problem. In this, what other people do to you or against you, it matters not, because you would have to take your eyes off of Him to see them anyway—and you can't.

Union

That they all may be one, as You, Father, are in Me, and I in You; that they also may be one in Us, that the world may believe that You sent Me

(John 17:21 NKJV).

To lay down upon His chest and feel His heart beating into your ear and charming your soul into alignment with His Person. To be able to be with Him is to walk in the midst of the garden of God and eat from the tree of life. I'm telling you this is what needs to be revived in your heart every single day. That is what the gospel of Christ does. We have been invited into the chambers of the King, to enjoy the sweet kisses of God.

You may well know all these things I have written to you in the pages of this book. But I pray that the Holy Spirit would again quicken you—that the Holy Spirit would again make the gospel real to you. I pray that Jesus would be beautiful again to you and that you would see that this is the most wonderful thing in the world—to be able to commune with the Man who is above all men.

He is the Man who has been raised from the dead, the firstborn among many brethren, who sits at the right hand of the throne of God, whose face is resplendent with glory, and who made John the Revelator absolutely powerless by just exposing the glory rays from His face to him.

I pray that, today, you would turn your eyes upon Jesus—that everything else would grow dim in the light of His glory. May your heart erupt in living communion with Him, creating such ease and simplicity in approaching Him. I pray that God Himself would remove burdens off your shoulders.

Union. Here is life's greatest joy, peace, satisfaction, success, and pleasure, whether we preach to millions or changes tires, whether our names are known or never heard of in this life. No one pleases God and carries the Kingdom of God into the earth like the person united with God, living a life of intimate communion.

About the Author

Eric Gilmour is an author, musician, and itinerant speaker who travels domestically and internationally. He and his wife, Brooke, are the founders of Sonship International—a teaching ministry committed to strengthening the Church. Their hearts are to bring the Church into a deeper experience of God's presence in their daily lives. With more than 100,000 subscribers on YouTube, Eric's music and teachings have aided millions of people in resting in the presence of God.

Eric, Brooke, and their two daughters, Madison and Lia, reside in Orlando, Florida. They have two golden retrievers, Mia and Oakley. When he's home you can find him spending time with his family, reading, or with a camera in his hand filming or taking pictures, namely in the golden hour.